CW00377242

WEST BROMWICH
ALBION
THE OFFICIAL ANNUAL 2009

A Grange Publication

Written by Dave Bowler

Designed by Colin Heggie

© 2008. Published by Grange Communications Ltd., Edinburgh,
under licence from West Bromwich Albion Football Club plc.
Printed in the EU.

Every effort has been made to ensure the accuracy of information within this publication but the
publishers cannot be held responsible for any errors or omissions. Views expressed are those
of the author and do not necessarily represent those of the publishers or the football club.
All rights reserved.

Photography by Laurie Rampling & Dave Bowler

Photographs © West Bromwich Albion Football Club Limited

ISBN 978-1-906211-47-9

£6.99

CONTENTS 2009

HE'S THE BOSS!

TONY MOWBRAY made his place in Albion history secure by leading the Throstles to Wembley for the second time inside 12 months and then by winning promotion – not bad in his first full season at the club!

The exciting, attacking style of play that Mowbray has brought to The Hawthorns is very different to the way he was as a player. Mowbray was a no-nonsense centre-half for Middlesbrough, Celtic and Ipswich but his teams are all about flair, excitement and attack – the Albion way of football.

Taking Albion into the Premier League is the biggest test of his career as a manager but after doing well against the might of Rangers and Celtic in the SPL when he was boss at Hibernian, there's no reason why he shouldn't succeed again.

So as the supporters so often sing, remember, "There's only one Tony Mowbray!"

WORD SEARCH

Jonathan Greening has lost some important Albion words — can you help him find these missing words in the grid?

```
P  K  K  U  D  G  B  F  R  J  K
H  A  W  T  H  O  R  N  S  K  O
I  J  E  Q  O  B  U  L  B  Z  R
L  A  B  L  E  O  N  M  D  O  E
L  L  S  T  F  H  T  N  M  F  N
I  V  C  H  K  L  O  A  B  U  K
P  I  G  R  E  E  N  I  N  G  G
S  T  L  N  N  B  U  N  A  R  E
D  Q  A  I  S  H  M  A  E  L  Z
F  E  G  M  V  Z  X  B  O  M  S
R  M  O  R  R  I  S  O  N  T  U
```

PHILLIPS	**HAWTHORNS**	**HOEFKENS**	**KOREN**	**GREENING**
MORRISON	**BRUNT**	**LEON**	**ISHMAEL**	**ROMAN**

Answers on p61

SEASON REVIEW

An unbelievable season, with an FA Cup semi-final, a day out at Wembley, promotion to the Premier League and finally, the Championship trophy itself.

So let manager Tony Mowbray take you behind the scenes and tell you just how we did it. . . .

There was a lot of change in the summer. We sold a lot of players but we got good money and managed to invest some of that back into the team which was a breath of fresh air. It created a good working environment out on the training ground and training was good and it was enthusiastic and it grew from pre-season really.

The dressing room needs to be pulling together to succeed, to be willing to go that extra inch. Regardless of how much individual talent you've got, if you don't have that togetherness you will struggle on wet, cold, horrible nights where teams might be playing direct against you and you've got to stick together and fight.

It's not all early season lush football pitches, us having the ball, spreading the pitch out and passing around teams. It's all types of football games and on the days when everybody's got to pull together, if you haven't got unity in the dressing room and there's one or two not fancying it, it's a problem because the ones who are working know the ones that aren't and that causes a bit of friction. On the first day at Burnley, we showed what a good football team we can be but there were still hangovers from last season, from a winning position we ended up losing the football match really. It was a bit like groundhog day that particular game and at Sheffield United. It was a scrappy game and a poor goal that we lost, but we didn't really function well enough as an attacking force that day. But sometimes defeats early on get the cob-webs out of the system because it allows everybody to express their own views, what's right and wrong. I didn't see it as a major problem but the two defeats away from home did raise that question of a soft underbelly and we had to address that.

Winning at Scunthorpe was important. They were newly promoted, a tight little ground, fans very, very close to the action. Maybe a year before we might have been hustled out of a game like that, too quick and frantic for us but we dominated the football match and

played some lovely stuff. Teixeira showed his true worth and his quality. We tried a different system that day of playing one striker and an attacking midfield behind him and it seemed to give them lots of problems, we scored goals, got the points and gave the team a bit of confidence to move on.

I was going through a period really where I was hoping to keep my whole back four in place, so they understand and develop together but it just didn't seem to be the case because one week, one player would be making big mistakes that cost us and then the following week it would be somebody else. So we were chopping and changing a little bit around the back four trying to get the right balance. Colchester was a very disappointing day for us, from a winning position finding ourselves losing the game almost comically really. We needed a lot of talking and organising to put

those things right and ultimately we did.

We got criticism for conceding goals, but if you try to score goals as we do, if you spread the team out a lot more, there's more space for the opposition if you give the ball away cheaply. We ask a lot of our defenders, to defend one against one. For me it's being brave, trying to win a football match sometimes at the expense of losing one. Away from home, maybe that's a lesson I've picked up over the last few months of the season, not being quite as expansive, playing one striker and flooding forward from midfield but being a lot more structured and solid.

Going to Watford was a big day and that win gave the players a great confidence. Beating the team at the top, we knew we could be competitive. Contrasting styles that day, Watford had battered their way to the top of the division, very forceful and

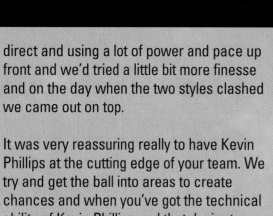

direct and using a lot of power and pace up front and we'd tried a little bit more finesse and on the day when the two styles clashed we came out on top.

It was very reassuring really to have Kevin Phillips at the cutting edge of your team. We try and get the ball into areas to create chances and when you've got the technical ability of Kevin Phillips and that desire to continue scoring goals then you've got a chance. Ishmael was really a wildcard in the transfer window but he came in and did so well from the start. Roman was different, he took six weeks to get himself fit but when Kevin and Ishmael got injured, he stepped in and carried on from there, he scored goals every time he went on the pitch and became a big favourite.

We had a lot of injuries and suspensions at Leicester and we could have felt sorry for ourselves. Shelton played at right-back and did exceptionally well, Jared on the left, Luke Steele in the goal but it showed the value of a squad of motivated players who've got something to prove. Ultimately Craig Beattie came and bent one in, a beautiful winner for us in the top corner and it was a sweet day, we enjoyed it.

At Christmas we hit some good goalscoring form. Bristol City thought they could come and take us on, they'd had some good results, but we put a performance on that would have been a handful for any side. And then we carried that on against Scunthorpe and scored five.

The cup run started in January and I was delighted to beat Charlton here. They scored very, very late to take it into extra time but what extra time showed me wasn't a team that felt sorry for themselves and got steamrollered by a resurgent Charlton. Instead, there was only one team who was going to win it in the extra time period. Great character by the team to bounce back from the disappointment and we got our rewards in the penalty shoot-out with Roman firing the winning penalty.

In the next round at Peterborough, we started very, very quickly, very well. We had a game plan and really overpowered them very early on. They'd been on a great run of form but with due respect, they were a League Two side and we needed to really impose ourselves on them. It was a professional job.

Barnsley away was a non event for us really, some shocking goals were conceded in front of a huge support that travelled to Barnsley. I felt as if we'd let them down but sometimes you need these games to take stock and to get a few home truths out, just to refocus the team. That Barnsley game did that because I mentioned it a few times in a few meetings in the coming months.

The FA Cup gave us momentum. There was a big crowd at Coventry, the Ricoh arena is a pretty imposing place when it's full so to go there and win 5-0 gave everybody a huge boost. It got the fans right behind the team, the team had an injection of self-confidence and belief and we were off and running to the end of the season.

Sheffield Wednesday was a game from the season before that stuck in my mind from a

few things that happened around the disappointment of that performance and that result. Personally, I was determined to go and try and get a positive result but it was a shocking pitch, a shocking night against a team fighting for their lives, a tremendous work ethic about them so to win so late was a wonderful feeling for the team and again one of those occasions that give the team a shot in the arm to keep believing.

Back in the cup, Bristol Rovers were the darlings of the media I suppose, the minnows that had gone so far in the competition but we went there with power and pace and a more direct style against them and outgunned them really. Ishmael scored a hat-trick and we came away 5-1 winners, delighted to get by what was potentially a tricky hurdle.

Leicester at home was a one off, a day where everything that could go wrong did go wrong. I remember saying to the players afterwards that of course it was disappointing but let's put it behind us very quickly, it's a one off. After that, Colchester was a classic case of needing strong characters in your team and the belief that we can score goals.

We had a spell where our deficiency from set plays had been highlighted, we'd worked on them a lot that week in training and yet as happens in football the first set play against us they score and then they score again with a well taken strike into the top corner and we find ourselves 2-0 down pretty early. I remember turning to Shakey next to me and saying "I think we'll still win this". We got two goals back and at half-time you think we've just got to go on and win it. The game became a lot tighter, yet they scored a breakaway goal, you're sitting losing the game, shaking your head at it, but thankfully we pulled out of it.

Losing to Portsmouth at Wembley was very disappointing. I was delighted with the way the team performed, delighted with the show that we put on for a huge audience, TV audience and the supporters. Putting it into perspective we were playing

Portsmouth who were sitting sixth in the Premier League and who were favourites to win the Cup and for long spells we were the better side. You've got to respect the defence they have, they won at Old Trafford 1-0, the week after they went to West Ham and won 1-0, they've kept a lot of clean sheets this year.

It was quite a change, from Wembley to Blackpool, a stadium with no stands behind two sides of the ground. Great credit to the players that they stuck with their job, we had to make a few changes in the game as we went along and ultimately they paid dividends. When we got the equaliser in that game, there was only one team that was going to win it. When we are playing on the front foot we can damage a lot of teams and we did that to Blackpool that night.

I think Wolves give us a chance to play because they try and play themselves. Whenever I've seen Wolves, when I've been studying them before we play them, they seem to dominate the football match, they're generally the better team but when they come up against our players they find they can't dominate, we tend to have slightly more of the ball than they do and it's a different type of match for them and ultimately we've come out on top.

Norwich showed two sides of the team. The first 20 minutes was almost a mismatch, we were on top and could have had plenty of goals. Then the last 20 minutes we needed to hang on and show defensive strength and togetherness in the team. The qualities were there for everybody to see, that we can play and hurt teams but we can also defend and be compact.

It wouldn't be Albion if we didn't make it slightly difficult for ourselves or give people a few nerves in the run-in. Against Southampton, in the second half especially, we did turn the gas up and pepper their goal and how we didn't score in that period is a bit of a mystery but then they go and hit you with a sucker punch ten minutes from the end and you're thinking that it's going to be one of those nights. But we kept going, got that crucial goal from Chris and it turned out to be a great occasion. To then retain the focus and clinch the title at QPR was testimony to the attitude of the players, but they thoroughly deserved it.

2007/08 **RESULTS**

DATE	OPPONENTS	RESULT	SCORERS
Sat 11 Aug	Burnley	1-2	Phillips
Tue 14 Aug	BOURNEMOUTH (LC1)	1-0	Beattie
Sat 18 Aug	PRESTON NORTH END	2-0	Phillips, Miller
Sat 25 Aug	Sheffield United	0-1	
Tue 28 Aug	Peterborough United (LC2)	2-0	Gera, Ellington
Sat 1 Sep	BARNSLEY	2-0	Teixeira, Beattie
Sat 15 Sep	IPSWICH TOWN	4-0	Miller, Teixeira, Phillips 2
Tue 18 Sep	Bristol City	1-1	Koren
Sat 22 Sep	Scunthorpe United	3-2	Barnett, Brunt, Teixeira
Tue 25 Sep	CARDIFF CITY (LC3)	2-4	Miller 2
Sun 30 Sep	QUEENS PARK RANGERS	5-1	Phillips 2, Miller, Koren, Greening
Wed 3 Oct	STOKE CITY	1-1	Barnett
Sat 6 Oct	Southampton	2-3	Koren 2
Sat 20 Oct	Colchester United	2-3	Phillips, Miller
Tue 23 Oct	BLACKPOOL	2-1	Miller, Morrison
Sat 27 Oct	NORWICH CITY	2-0	Miller, Phillips
Sat 3 Nov	Watford	3-0	Miller, Phillips, Albrechtsen
Tue 6 Nov	SHEFFIELD WEDNESDAY	1-1	Phillips
Mon 12 Nov	Coventry City	4-0	Robinson, Teixeira 2, Koren
Sun 25 Nov	WOLVES	0-0	
Wed 28 Nov	Plymouth Argyle	2-1	Bednar 2
Sat 1 Dec	Crystal Palace	1-1	Hudson (og)
Tue 4 Dec	COVENTRY CITY	2-4	Bednar 2
Sat 8 Dec	Leicester City	2-1	Gera, Beattie
Sat 15 Dec	CHARLTON ATHLETIC	4-2	Bednar, Gera2, Phillips
Sat 22 Dec	Stoke City	1-3	Bednar
Wed 26 Dec	BRISTOL CITY	4-1	Bednar, Koren, Phillips 2
Sat 29 Dec	SCUNTHORPE UNITED	5-0	Phillips 2, Koren, Gera, Beattie
Tue 1 Jan	Ipswich Town	0-2	
Sat 5 Jan	Charlton Athletic (FAC3)	1-1	Miller
Sat 12 Jan	Hull City	3-1	Phillips, Morrison, Bednar
Tue 15 Jan	CHARLTON ATHLETIC (FAC3)	2-2	Bednar, Morrison
		(won 4-3 on penalties)	
Sat 19 Jan	CARDIFF CITY	3-3	Bednar, Albrechtsen, Johnson (og)
Sat 26 Jan	Peterborough United (FAC4)	3-0	Bednar, Koren, Phillips
Tue 29 Jan	Preston North End	1-2	Gera
Sat 2 Feb	BURNLEY	2-1	Cesar, Bednar
Sat 9 Feb	Barnsley	1-2	Morrison
Tue 12 Feb	SHEFFIELD UNITED	0-0	
Sat 16 Feb	Coventry City (FAC5)	5-0	Brunt, Bednar 2, Miller, Gera
Sat 23 Feb	HULL CITY	1-2	Bednar
Sat 1 Mar	PLYMOUTH ARGYLE	3-0	Gera, Miller, Bednar
Tue 4 Mar	Sheffield Wednesday	1-0	Phillips
Sun 9 Mar	Bristol Rovers (FAC6)	5-1	Morrison, Miller 3, Phillips
Wed 12 Mar	CRYSTAL PALACE	1-1	Phillips
Sat 15 Mar	LEICESTER CITY	1-4	Koren
Fri 21 Mar	Charlton Athletic	1-1	Phillips
Sat 29 Mar	COLCHESTER UNITED	4-3	Phillips, Brunt, Morrison, Bednar
Tue 1 Apr	Cardiff City	0-0	
Sat 5 Apr	Portsmouth (FAC SF)	0-1	
Tue 8 Apr	Blackpool	3-1	Phillips 2, Miller
Sat 12 Apr	WATFORD	1-1	Barnett
Tue 15 Apr	Wolves	1-0	Gera
Sat 19 Apr	Norwich City	2-1	Koren, Gera
Sat 26 Apr	SOUTHAMPTON	1-1	Brunt
Sun 4 May	Queens Park Rangers	2-0	Kim, Brunt

Bird BRAIN!

We all know that the Albion are the Throstles — as represented by the Baggie Birds — but in the Championship, we came across some other teams who have a bird as their nickname.

Do you recognise the teams in the pictures?

And do you know their nicknames?

Answers on p61

CYRILLE REGIS **MBE!**

Albion legend Cyrille Regis popped up in the Queen's Birthday Honours List last June, being rewarded for his "services to the voluntary sector and to football" with an MBE.

CYRILLE PLAYED for the Throstles between 1977 and 1984 and was voted as West Bromwich Albion's all time Cult Hero in a BBC Sport poll, gaining 65 per cent of the vote. In the same year he was named as one of Albion's 16 greatest players, in a poll organised as part of the club's 125th anniversary celebrations.

Cyrille was delighted with the award and said, "It's fantastic to be awarded an MBE and I'm absolutely delighted. It makes you think about your mum and dad, your children, your mentors, managers, fans and everyone who has played their part in my life and career."

Keep your eyes on future honours lists – it can't be long before he's made the Lord of West Bromwich!

JUST ANSWER THE QUESTION: CHRIS BRUNT

What is your favourite item of clothing?
I don't have that many good ones! It's hard to say, but I'm going to go for trainers as I buy quite a few pairs.

What is your favourite colour?
Blue. I don't know why, it just is, ever since I was a kid I just liked it.

What was your best and worst subject at school?
My best subject was probably French, I got an A* in my GSCE, I can't remember any of it now though. I was quite good at languages, my sister is studying French and Spanish at university and my Mum was good at languages too, so I think it must run in the family. My worst subject was probably computing, I just didn't like it at school, and I found it a bit boring.

When was the last time you used public transport?
I went to watch a concert at Sheffield Arena, which is not far from my mate's house. Four of us went in on the tram. That was in May. We went to go and see Lionel Richie, he was brilliant, and I saw him the year before as well.

What is your favourite computer game?
I don't play on the computer an awful lot now. I used to play a lot when I was in my digs in Middlesbrough. The only computer game I do play now is ProEvolution Soccer, which I play with my brother when I go home.

If you were cooking to impress, what dish would you select?
I'm not a great cook, so I'd probably cook some basic stuff, maybe some kind of pasta. Although, I did stretch to Fajitas one time, but I think I'd have to stick to the pasta.

If you could buy a ticket to any event in the world, what would it be?
Probably the World Cup Final. I wouldn't mind who was playing, it would just be great to be there in the stands. Mind you, I would obviously like to be there supporting Northern Ireland, I wouldn't care who they were playing. It could be anybody, as long as they were in the final!

Would you rather be a Cowboy or a Red Indian?
I'd say an Indian because I'd rather have a bow and arrow than a gun. I think you'd have to use a bit more skill with a bow and arrow.

What keeps you awake at night?
Not much really, I don't usually have much trouble getting to sleep. Like most people, if there is something on your mind it can trouble you and you stay awake, but generally I'm okay.

BETWEEN the STICKS

Albion have had plenty of great goalkeepers down the years but we've been especially blessed with a number of long term custodians over the last 40 years or so.

John Osborne was our FA Cup winning goalkeeper in 1968 when he was an inspiration to the side, on the pitch and off it too – he was a quiz league champion back in the days when Albion used to win the Quiz Ball competition on the BBC – ask your granddad!

Tony Godden succeeded Ossie in goal in the 1970s and 1980s and had a number of great seasons behind the defence of Batson, Statham, Wile and Robertson as we took the Albion name out into Europe and to the top of the league as well.

Russell Hoult holds the record for the most clean sheets in a season for the Albion, keeping the opposition out in the 2001/2 promotion season, the famous year of "1-0 to the Albion!"

Dean Kiely is our latest promotion winning 'keeper, and the Golden Gloves winner in the Championship last term for posting the most clean sheets in the division, earning a recall to the Ireland squad into the bargain!

BEATING AROUND THE BUSH!

Albion's Championship winning season ended in London's Shepherds Bush when we beat QPR 2-0 to clinch the title.

And we did it in style, even if the fashion police might have wanted a word with one or two of our supporters. ....

CROSSWORD

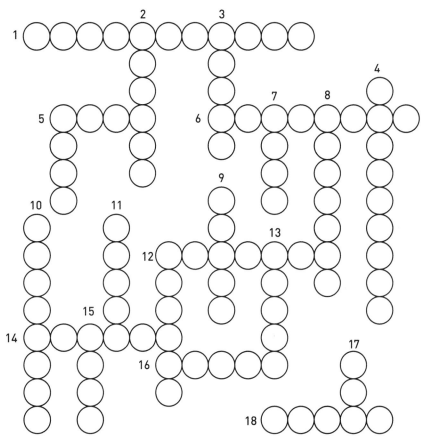

ACROSS

1 He's the boss!
5 Robbo's first name.
6 The last Albion captain to lift the FA Cup. Graham _____
12 The end of the ground where most home fans sit.
14 If you have one of these tickets, you can get into every home game.
16 There are gates in his honour at The Hawthorns.
18 Bednar's first name – but he isn't Italian!

DOWN

2 Surname of the goalscorer we bought from Manchester City.
3 Albion's record goalscorer. Tony _____
4 The end of the ground where home and away fans sit.
5 The former Southampton man or Brazil's greatest footballer?
7 Mr Barnett.
8 First name of 2 down.
9 Scored the goal that sealed promotion.
10 There's a model of this bird in the Woodman Corner.
11 The assistant manager.
12 Albion's striker is Czech, not Italian!
13 Luke _____ joined us from Villa.
15 Half the league games are at home and half are _____
17 Who are we?

ANSWERS ON P61

JUST ANSWER THE QUESTION: CARL HOEFKENS

What is your favourite ice-cream?
Vanilla. Just normal, standard vanilla. I don't like all the fancy ice-cream.

What was the last album you downloaded to your iPod?
I think it was the last one by Eminem, which would have been ages ago. My iPod is completely full and as the music is quite good, I probably won't download anything for a while.

Who would play you in the film of your life?
I'd go for Hugh Jackman who was Wolverine in X-Men. Everyone said I looked liked him!

What was your best and worst subject at school?
My best was languages. It didn't really matter which one. My worst was maths. I hated maths. It was horrible.

What keeps you awake at night?
A bad smell! I'm quite a good sleeper and I'm not a person who worries too much. But sometimes, if something is on my mind, I might keep thinking about it. Probably the only thing that would keep me awake would be trouble with my family.

What is your favourite item of clothing?
My absolute favourite is just jeans and a T-shirt because they're comfy. I'm not one for dressing up a lot for parties and things like that. I do sometimes, but I prefer just being casual.

What is your greatest achievement in football?
In my second season at Germinal Beerschot, we won the cup in the final against Bruges, who were then champions of Belgium. Being in the national team at the age of 18, and also playing first-team football at the age of 17, wasn't too bad either.

What is your favourite goal you have scored?
Probably my favourite was against Sporting Lisbon in the Champions League, when I was with Lierse, who are a small side in Belgium.

Have you any pre-match rituals?
The only thing I do is take to the pitch with my right foot and come off it with my left. I don't know if that counts as a ritual, though. I'm not even sure why I do it!

When was the last time you used public transport?
It was most likely when I was at college in Belgium. I caught the bus a lot then. That's not counting the Euro Tunnel, which I use a lot when I go home.

the BIG QUIZ

1 Who scored Albion's first goal of the Championship winning season?

2 And who scored the last?

3 Which club did Darren Carter join from Albion?

4 And where did Richard Chaplow go?

5 Which country does Dean Kiely represent?

6 Where did Tony Mowbray start his playing career?

7 Who scored Albion's first ever Premier League goal?

8 When was the last time the Throstles lifted the League Championship trophy?

9 Who has scored the most goals for Albion?

10 Who was the last Albion player to score at Wembley in a first team game?

11 Who was Albion's first full-time player-manager?

12 And who was the second?

13 Which club did Neil Clement join the Throstles from?

14 What is the name of Luke Moore's footballing brother?

15 Who were Albion's three degrees?

16 Which famous guitarist once featured an Albion scarf on an album cover?

17 What was the original name of the team?

18 What year was The Hawthorns opened?

19 Carl Hoefkens comes from which European country?

20 Which Albion fan presents the BBC's "One Show"?

ANSWERS ON P61

DEFENDER OF THE FAITH!

Albion broke the bank in the summer to buy Gianni Zuiverloon from Dutch club Heerenveen, spending £3.2million on the Dutch Olympic and Under-21 star, the most we've ever paid for a right-back.

Gianni played in the Dutch Under 21 team that won the European Championships in 2007, and is now looking to progress his career by playing in the Premier League. "It's a nice club, I want to play in the Premier League and they've given me a chance. I know Tony Mowbray is a good trainer. He knows what he wants and he is a very honest man.

"The training facilities are good and the stadium is really nice. It's my dream to play against the big names in the Premier League and now I'm finally here. I feel I am a good defender and I also get forward to get crosses in. I'm very excited to begin and show everyone who I am.

"I spoke to my good friend from Liverpool, Ryan Babel, and he said this was a big step for me and I will be alright. I always played against Ryan in the Dutch league and I always said to him I was going to play against him in the Premier League. Now it's finally there and it's a big chance for me. I hope I can adapt to the Premier League as well as Ryan has. I want to prove myself and get better like he did as the season went on."

Gianni owes his success to his Mum, who started him off on his career by getting him a trial at Feyenoord as a five year old!
"My mum just picked Feyenoord's number out of the phonebook and rang them. She didn't know anything about football. I went for a trial and they signed me. It was a very good place to develop as a footballer, you're brought up playing football at Feyenoord.

"I looked at the style of play that Albion use before making my decision to come here because I didn't want to play for a team that just uses the long ball. West Brom like to play football, which suits me."

ISHMAEL MILLER Falling over in a night club probably, but everyone has done that!

LEON BARNETT Turning up late to training when I had just started here, with all the boys seeing me and laughing! I was 30 minutes late so I got quite a big fine.

JAMES MORRISON Probably when I was at Middlesbrough. When I was about 17, we didn't clean the boots, so we were made to sing a song in front of the first team. I think we sung the Hokey-Cokey! That was very embarrassing.

how **EMBARRASSING**

We asked some of Albion's finest, "Just what was your most embarrassing moment?" Here's what they came up with!

NEIL CLEMENT When I was about 19 at Chelsea I was a member of this gym. I used to go in the afternoons. I was there one day doing some running on the treadmill and my towel, which was balancing on the side, fell on the treadmill and landed half on it and half off it. I tried to scoop it up as I was running but I slipped and literally did a somersault and landed on the floor! All the gym instructors came running over panicking. It was packed as well. Everyone was just gawping at me. That was pretty embarrassing!

JONATHAN GREENING Probably getting my bum slapped by Paul Robinson in front of a lot of people on a beach in Marbella after losing a game of football!

GOALS **GOALS** GOALS!

Nobody scores goals like Albion scored goals last season.

109 of them in all competitions on the way to the Football League Championship and the FA Cup semi-final — so many we couldn't fit them all in!

But here are a few of the very best — do you remember them?

sign HERE!

Baggie Bird has collected some Albion autographs for you, but he can't remember which signature goes with which player!

Can you help him out?

1

2

3

4

5

Answers on p61

the men AT THE BACK

Since the war, the Throstles have been able to call on a string of great defenders to help the cause, the line going all the way back to Belfast-born Jack Vernon who was our main man in defence for five seasons before he returned home to Northern Ireland.

John Kaye, a former centre-forward, completely changed his job description in 1968 and did it so well that he was the centre-half in the team that beat Everton to win the FA Cup at Wembley that year!

Many think Derek Statham is one of the greatest players ever to wear the stripes. He played his part in Ron Atkinson's great team of the late 1970s and 1980s, a left-back who played more like a winger at times, dashing forward to join in with the attack, but quick enough to get back into defence when he had to.

Larus Sigurdsson, the Ice Man from Iceland, was a very important figure in the team that won promotion to the Premier League for the first time as part of the three man central defence with Phil Gilchrist and Darren Moore. Nobody in their right mind ever upset Siggy!

Then there's Neil Clement, the first ever Albion player to win three promotions. Clem has played all over the back line, at wing-back, left-back and centre-half and with 300 games behind him, he's a real Albion legend.

IN SAFE HANDS!

If ever you want to show the world that you mean business as a new club to the Premier League, there aren't many better ways of going about it than buying yourself an England goalkeeper!

Former Liverpool man Scott Carson joined the club in July for £3.25million, and he's a 'keeper with a huge future ahead of him. He stands second in the all-time list of England Under-21 appearance-makers with 29 to his name, and already has two full international caps at the age of 22.

But it's his Albion future that he has on his mind, not England.

"The main thing is trying to have a good season here and stay in the Premier League. This is the most important season. If we can have a good season this year then we can push on and hopefully look further up the table.

"England is always at the back of my mind. I want to get back into that set up but first and foremost it's about getting games for West Brom.

"I think players have got more chance of getting in the England team if they're playing regularly rather than sitting on the bench and playing only ten games for Manchester United, Liverpool or Chelsea. If regular football wasn't going to come for me at Liverpool, I wasn't prepared to sit there and just pick up my money.

"I've come here to try and play every week and hopefully move my career on. Some players are happy to just pick up wages but for the last three-and-a-half years I've gone out on loan when it would have been easy to sit on the bench at Liverpool.

"It wasn't an easy decision to leave a massive club like Liverpool. But when West Brom showed their interest and, after speaking to the manager, I just thought 'this is the right move for me'.

"It's great to be part of the club. Having spoken to the manager, and seen the way he's going, I think there's going to be a good future here."

Albion are used to having a young England goalkeeper at the club because back in 2005/6, Chris Kirkland spent a year on loan at The Hawthorns – also joining us from Liverpool.

"I spent around six months with Chris at Liverpool. They signed me after Chris got injured, so we only trained a couple of times together at Liverpool but I know him quite well through England duty.

"I spoke to him a few times before signing because he's been here and knows this place. He said he really enjoyed his time at Albion and spoke really highly of Joe Corrigan, the goalkeeping coach, and the people here.

"Everyone I spoke to about West Brom last year said they were the best footballing side in the Championship and deserved to get back into the Premier League.

"Obviously it's a big step into the Premier League but I'm confident, having spoken to the manager and seen the players that are at the club, we can have a good season.

"It's a big weight off my mind knowing that I'm going to be at a club for the next four or five years and maybe even longer. It's not easy going to a club for just one season. By the time you settle in, it's time to leave. Hopefully I can get settled here really quickly, get back to playing football, get a good run in the team and find some consistency in my game.

"I've got two full seasons of Premier League games under my belt and I know what it's about. It's going to be difficult but now it's about taking those last two seasons and using them to my advantage to hopefully push on."

IMPROVE YOUR SKILLS

WEST BROMWICH ALBION

WITH JONATHAN GREENING!
1V1 FACING AN OPPONENT SIDESTEP

THE MOVE:

The player fakes to pass the ball with the outside of the foot but instead steps behind the ball and takes it in the opposite direction with the outside of the other foot.

COACHING POINTS:

- Use eyes and communication to disguise the pass
- Exaggerate upper body movement to deceive and unbalance the opponent
- Short step behind the ball is all that is required

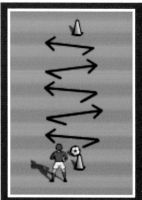

SKILL PRACTICE 1

- Players work moving forward in between the 2 cones practicing the side step move.
- Step right – go left
- Step left – go right
- See how many moves you can perform and try to beat your record.

SKILL PRACTICE 2

- Dribble forward to cones and perform the left go right side step then drive forward to opposite cone.
- Repeat exercise this time performing the right go left move.
- Progression – try double side step
- Step right – left – right
- Step left – right – left

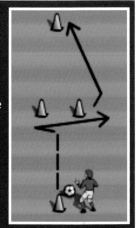

PLAYERS MUST BE AWARE OF THE VARIOUS SITUATIONS ON THE PARK

WHERE & WHEN THE MOVE CAN BE BEST EXECUTED:

- STRIKER – When in or around the box and confronted with a defender face to face, using a quick side step move will allow you to create space to finish on goal.

- MIDFIELDER – When attacking at an angle from a wide midfield position and being faced with an opponent, a quick side step move will allow you to create space for a penetrating pass, a cross or shot at goal.

- DEFENDER – When being faced by an opponent in a defending area performing a quick side step move will allow you space to set up a forward pass into midfielder/ striker or winger enabling you to set up an attack from a defensive situation.

WITH ROBERT KOREN!
1V1 SIDE BY SIDE (STOP TURN)

THE MOVE:
The Player dribbles forward jumps over the ball and stops ball with sole of the foot. After landing beyond the ball turn quickly and take the ball away in the opposite direction.

Practice this move at least 10 times each day for a minimum of 5 days a week.

COACHING POINTS:
* Do not hesitate when jumping over the ball
* Use light touch with the sole of the foot when stopping the ball
* After changing direction accelerate out of the move

SKILL PRACTICE
* In this practice the 2 cones in the middle act as the opposing players.
* To start, dribble with the ball to the 3rd cone where the player is on your right hand side.
* Perform the left foot turn to change direction.
* Then dribble back to the 2nd cone and change direction again this time using the right foot turn.
* Once you have performed the turn dribble forward to the 4th cone and repeat practice.

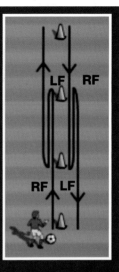

TO USE THIS MOVE EFFECTIVELY IT HAS TO BE PRACTICED REGULARLY WITH BOTH FEET

WHERE & WHEN THE MOVE CAN BE BEST EXECUTED:
* STRIKER – driving across edge of the box with opponent side by side performs the turn to create space for shot at goal.
* MIDFIELDER – driving across midfield can change direction quickly to switch play or pass to striker to create opening.
* DEFENDER – running back towards own goal under pressure from opposition can change direction quickly to create space and start attacking.

WITH ISHMAEL MILLER! 1V1 DIAGONAL ATTACK DRAG BACK

THE MOVE:
When being challenged from the side fake to strike the ball but instead drag the ball back with the sole of the same foot and push off in the opposite direction using the inside or outside of the drag back foot.

COACHING POINTS:
* Exaggerate the fake strike of the ball
* Drag back must be executed quickly
* Get ball out of feet to clear the incoming opponent
* To be successful the timing of the move is crucial

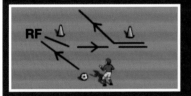

SKILL PRACTICE 1
* Dribble the ball slightly past the left hand cone and perform the right foot (RF) drag back move.
* Then dribble across to the other cone and perform the left foot (LF) drag back. Dribble through the middle of the two cones.
* Stop the ball and repeat the practice.

SKILL PRACTICE 2
* Start at the first cone by performing the right foot (RF) drag back.
* Proceed to the second cone and perform the left foot (LF) drag back.
* Continue up the circuit using the right foot and left foot drag back move.

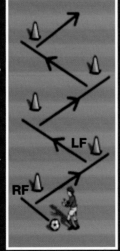

PLAYERS MUST BE AWARE OF THE VARIOUS SITUATIONS ON THE PARK

WHERE & WHEN THE MOVE CAN BE BEST EXECUTED:
* STRIKER – When driving forward into the box and being challenged diagonally from the side using the drag back move will allow the player to create space to beat the defender, creating an opportunity to finish on goal.
* MIDFIELDER – When dribbling forward in a midfield position and being challenged diagonally from the side, quickly performing the drag back move will allow the player to create space for a pass into the striker or wide player.
* DEFENDER – When in possession of the ball outside the penalty box and facing your own goal the drag back move would be a good option when being challenged from the side. The move would allow the player to create space and take the ball clear of the danger zone.

the ENGINE ROOM

Every football manager will tell you that games are won and lost in the middle of the park, and the reason Albion have such a proud history is that we've had some of the finest middle men of them all at the club over the years.

Perhaps the greatest of them all was Ray Barlow, member of the great Albion side that won the FA Cup and finished second in the league in 1954. Sir Bobby Robson called him one of the finest passers of the ball he's ever seen, and compliments don't come much higher than that!

If Barlow was the best passer, Bobby Hope must run him a close second! Playmaker in the Throstles' midfield when we won the FA Cup in 1968, Bobby remains an all-time Albion great, and still works at the club as a major part of our scouting operation.

Bryan Robson went on to become England's Captain Marvel after he left the Baggies, but in his formative years at The Hawthorns, Bryan played a lot of the best football of his career, regularly being man of the match – no mean feat in a side that included Regis, Cunningham, Statham, Tony Brown, Cantello, Wile and Robertson!

Derek McInnes was a driving force in the engine room of the team that went on to win promotion to the Premier League for the first time. An inspirational captain and a great ball winner in the centre of the field, Derek won his Scotland caps while an Albion player too.

Over the last couple of years, Robert Koren has become a big favourite at The Hawthorns with his energetic work in midfield, as well as the ten goals that he scored for the Throstles in last season's Championship winning campaign.

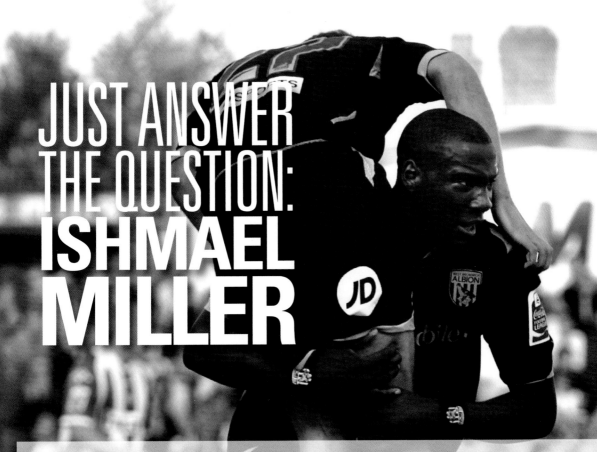

JUST ANSWER THE QUESTION: ISHMAEL MILLER

Which team did you support as a boy?
Manchester City of course.

Who did you have a schoolboy crush on?
Jennifer Lopez, I still do. She is fit!

What was your best and worst subject at school?
My best was PE, I got an A*. My worst was Spanish; I dropped out because I was so rubbish at it.

If you could buy a ticket to any event in the world, what would it be?
NBA final as I'm quite a big basketball fan. I would love to see Miami Heat and LA Lakers in the final.

When was the last time you used public transport?
Probably about four years ago when I went on a bus.

What would your superpower be?
I'd like to be able to read minds so I'd know what people are thinking all the time.

What is your favourite ice-cream?
Strawberry, I don't mind what make as long as it's Strawberry.

Property aside, what is the most expensive thing you have bought?
My car. It's a BMW six series convertible.

What is your most treasured possession?
Probably my car.

Who is your favourite cartoon character?
Spiderman because his costume is good. I love cartoons!

What is your greatest achievement in football?
When I scored my first goal in professional football here at West Brom. It was an alright goal as well, so that would be my biggest achievement so far.

What is your favourite colour?
Baby blue, I don't know why, I just like it.

What is your favourite computer game?
Pro-Evolution Soccer on the Xbox. It's the best.

HOME SWEET HOME!

THE THROSTLES have played at The Hawthorns for more than 100 years now – our ground was the first new Football League stadium of the 20th century, opened on 3rd September 1900. The first game was a 1-1 draw with Derby, their Steve Bloomer scoring the first goal at the ground, Chippy Simmons becoming Albion's first scorer.

You could only get 35,000 people in the ground back then but by 1924, capacity had nearly doubled to 65,000 as going to football became more and more popular – you couldn't watch it on TV back then!

Night games didn't start to happen until the 1950s, Albion installing floodlights in 1957 at a cost of £18,000, the first floodlit game a 1-1 draw with Chelsea on 18th September 1957. The lights were also used for a cricket game in 1980 when a Warwickshire XI played Ian Botham's XI in aid of Alistair Robertson's testimonial!

The Rainbow Stand – which stood where the East Stand now is – was built in 1964 and was called the Rainbow because of its multicoloured seats. In 1976, in front of the Rainbow, we built our very first executive boxes, a sign of the times.

Halfords Lane was the next to be changed, and between 1979 and 1982, the existing structure was put in place, featuring seats, a press box and director's box, along with 26 more executive boxes. The Taylor Report meant we needed to put

seats in the Brummie and Smethwick Ends, the stands at either end of the ground completely replaced at a cost of £4.15million. The first game at the all-seater Hawthorns was against Bristol City on 26th December 1995, Albion winning 1-0.

The Rainbow Stand had outlived its usefulness and that whole side of the ground was demolished in 2001 to make way for the £7.5million East Stand which is still the main stand at The Hawthorns.

The Halfords Lane Stand was extensively modernized in 2008 and is now known as the West Stand, with the director's box having moved back to that side of the ground.

The Hawthorns is a famous ground not just because of the many great Albion games that have been played there but because it is the highest Football League ground in the country, at 551 feet above sea level.

Albion were also the first club in the country to use the stilecard ticketing system in 2002, also becoming the first club to use big screens in widescreen format at the same time.

So next time you come to The Hawthorns remember – you're coming to an historic place!

CAPTAIN MARVEL!

It was former Albion midfielder Bryan Robson that was christened "Captain Marvel" after he took the captain's armband for the England team, but after his performances in Albion's Championship winning season, it's Jonathan Greening who deserves the title these days!

Jono was a surprise selection to be Albion captain when Tony Mowbray gave him the job, but throughout the season, he grew into the role more and more and by season's end, he was playing the part like a natural.

Team mate Carl Hoefkens is a big fan, saying, "All his brains are in his feet! He's got amazing feet, he can do everything he wants with the ball. I think the manager made a great move by putting him in central midfield, he loves to play there and it's a great thing to play as a full-back because if you haven't got an option to play forward he's always available. He never loses the ball. The way he does the captaincy, you have to give him a lot of credit for that, he is very easy, very relaxed and I've got loads of respect for him."

Jono played every league game last season and overall, there was just the one match he missed, due to suspension – the FA Cup win at Coventry. As Albion's playmaker as well as the club captain, Greening had to shoulder a lot of responsibility but his form was never less than excellent.

Although Kevin Phillips' goals took most of the headlines, Jono's contribution to the cause was massive, making him many people's choice as Albion's most influential player in the Championship.

"Maybe with age you feel more responsible for your team-mates so I think I've matured that way," he said. "Going out on the pitch you try and not just think about your game but try and think about others, encouraging or telling people off if they need it. It's the same before games, speaking in front of everybody - people tell me to shut up now which is quite nice!"

which**WAY**?

Luke Moore hasn't been with Albion long, and he still can't work out how to get from the training ground to The Hawthorns.

Can you help him find the way?

Answers on p61

CECH IN!

After Albion bought in Gianni Zuiverloon as competition on the right of defence, it was only correct that we balance things up and get ourselves another left-back!

Marek Cech was the man, joining us for £1.4million in the summer. The Slovakian international joined us from Porto, where he had won the league for the last three years in a row and played in the Champions League.

"The interest in me from West Brom was so strong," revealed Cech, who speaks fluent English. "I appreciated it and I was very happy about it, that's why I chose this club.

"It is a big challenge for me to prove myself in the Premier League. Now I will be playing in the most interesting league in the world and I want to show myself in a good light.

"I like to play attacking football because it's nice for the supporters to watch. It is also more interesting for the players. Everybody here wants to win and attack - and I like to attack.

"A few days ago I was shown around the training centre and the stadium and I was really surprised about how good the facilities are. The people at the club were also very nice to me."

So here's one Cech that's boinging instead of bouncing!

GOAL !!!!!!

We go to games to see the goals flood in, and Albion have had some real goalscoring legends over the seasons.

Ronnie Allen was known as "the complete footballer" in his hey day in the 1950s when he scored more than 200 goals for the Throstles, collected an FA Cup winners' medal and played for England too.

Allen's goalscoring record lasted until the 1970s when the Albion's all-time great, Tony Brown, sailed past it. "Bomber" also holds the record for most appearances for the club and pretty well every other record you can think of.
Tony is Mr Albion, and remains a great servant, writing in the matchday programme and covering every game, home and away, for local radio.

Bomber's great partner in goals was Jeff Astle, "The King", who scored the winner in the 1954 FA Cup Final to write himself into Albion folklore for ever more. Few players have ever been more popular with the Albion fans than Astle and his legacy was marked by the installation of the Astle gates on the Brummie Road.

Of more recent vintage, Super Bob Taylor made an otherwise miserable decade much more enjoyable with his string of goals through the 1990s. Bob left for Bolton at one point, but returned in triumph, first to save the club from relegation and then to steer it to promotion to the Premier League with bags of goals for the Baggies!

Roman Bednar is the latest goalscoring hero, the Czech striker coming down from Hearts to score almost a goal a game as Albion powered on to the Championship title last term, a real Roman conquest!

JUST ANSWER THE QUESTION:
JAMES MORRISON

What was the last album you downloaded to your iPod?
It was the new Jay-Z one, American Gangster, which is good. I like Jay-Z. I'm not a massive fan but I have got a couple of his albums.

Property aside, what is the most expensive thing you have bought?
A Cartier watch. That cost a few bob!

Which words or phrases do you most overuse?
Nerd! I mainly just say that to Jono Greening which may not be a surprise!

Who was your hero as a youngster?
I had quite a few footballers as heroes, to be honest: Paul Gascoigne, David Beckham, Roy Keane, Paul Ince, Eric Cantona. Pretty much all out-and-out footballers.

Which team did you support as a boy?
Manchester United. I don't really follow them now, although all my mates still do. I tend to support the other team when I watch them play with my mates, just to give them a bit of aggro!

When was the last time you used public transport?
I use it quite often, actually. I tend to get the train back home to Darlington a lot. The last time was about two weeks ago. It's a lot easier than being stuck in traffic. I hate traffic!

If you were cooking to impress, what dish would you select?
If I could cook, I might start with a prawn cocktail, then a salad with a bit of Salmon, maybe, or just some kind of meat, then a nice little treacle pudding to finish, as that's my favourite. I don't think anyone would be too excited by that menu, though!

What is your favourite ice-cream?
I've got two: vanilla and strawberry, plain and simple. I like the Haagen Dazs vanilla. For strawberry I'd have to say Wall's! I do like Mr Whippy from ice-cream vans too. Actually, I was in Jimmy Spices not long ago and, for pudding, I had the ice-cream because it was like the Mr Whippy stuff. I had to put it in the cone myself. It's not easy you know!

What is your most treasured possession?
I'm not sure, maybe my jewellery and football shirts from games I have played in. I've collected quite a few over the years like Frank Lampard's and Wayne Rooney's.

What is your greatest achievement in football?
Playing in three finals stands out. The UEFA Cup final with Middlesbrough in 2006 against Sevilla, the FA Youth Cup final for Boro in 2004 when we won 4-0 against Villa, and the European Championships Under-19s final in 2005. I was also the first person to score in European competition for Middlesbrough.

PLAYER PROFILES

CARL HOEFKENS
BORN: 6 OCTOBER 1978
POSITION: FULL-BACK
ALBION APPEARANCES: 47

Carl joined from Stoke in 2007 and was a virtual ever present in the team in the run through to promotion, going from a Jonathan Greening lookalike to a Wolverine stand in!

Carl didn't catch the eye just because of his changing hairstyles but because of his attacking style at right-back, often getting forward to offer another threat, playing almost as a winger at times. A Belgian international, Carl has also played in the Champions League.

PAUL ROBINSON

BORN: 14 DECEMBER 1978
POSITION: FULL-BACK
ALBION APPEARANCES: 198+3 SUB
ALBION GOALS: 4

Robbo spent last season getting into plenty of scrapes with his all action style, so much so that he got the nickname Mr Bump because of the number of times he had to play with a bandage on his head!

Another who hardly missed a game in the promotion campaign, this will be Robbo's third Premiership season with the Throstles, to add to the one he enjoyed earlier in his career with Watford.

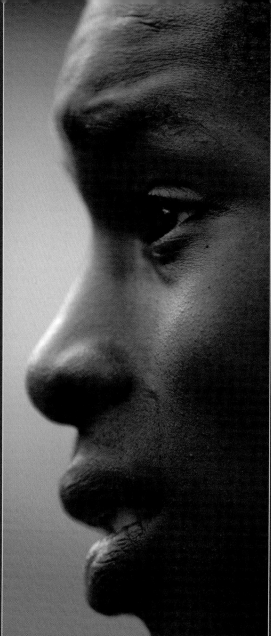

LEON BARNETT

BORN: 30 NOVEMBER 1985
POSITION: CENTRE-HALF
ALBION APPEARANCES: 34+2 SUB
ALBION GOALS: 4

Leon was a £2.5million signing from Luton Town as Tony Mowbray rebuilt his squad ahead of last season, and he quickly slotted into the centre of the Albion defence.

Still relatively inexperienced, Leon played plenty of games for the Baggies last season and got better and better as the season went on, earning his chance to play against the best in the world in the Premier League this season.

NEIL CLEMENT

BORN: 3 OCTOBER 1978
POSITION: CENTRE-HALF
ALBION APPEARANCES: 275+25 SUB
ALBION GOALS: 26

The longest serving player at The Hawthorns, there are few more popular than Clem and everyone was delighted to see him back from a couple of years of injury problems to play a big part in the promotion push.

Clem has played as both a wing-back and a centre-half for Albion over his eight years at the club and he has also scored plenty of important goals, mostly with his wand of a left foot from free-kicks just outside the box.

GIANNI ZUIVERLOON

BORN: 30 DECEMBER 1986
POSITION: FULL-BACK
ALBION APPEARANCES: 0

Zuiverloon joined Albion from Heerenveen in the summer in a £3.2million transfer that makes him the club's most expensive defender ever – he first caught the eye when Heerenveen played a friendly at The Hawthorns in August 2007.

That appearance came after he had played a part in the Dutch Under 21 team that won the European Championships on home soil in 2007, Zuiverloon scoring the winning penalty in the shootout that knocked England out of the competition – Gianni took the 32nd penalty of the marathon shootout and won the game for his country.

JAMES MORRISON
BORN: 25 MAY 1986
POSITION: MIDFIELDER
ALBION APPEARANCES: 32+11 SUB
ALBION GOALS: 6

James joined Albion in the summer of 2007 for a bargain £1.5million and made his mark on the team throughout the promotion campaign with a series of energetic and assured performances in the midfield, playing on either wing and through the middle.

A hard worker with a good range of passing and someone who can chip in with important goals, James is a key member of Tony Mowbray's team. James has played for England right through to Under-20 level, but has chosen to play full international football for Scotland, qualifying through his grandparents.

JONATHAN GREENING
BORN: 2 JANUARY 1979
POSITION: MIDFIELDER
ALBION APPEARANCES: 176+8 SUB
ALBION GOALS: 6

Albion's Captain Fantastic last season, Jonathan led the team from the front through to promotion. Playing in the centre of midfield, he was the team's playmaker with most of our football going through him.

He rarely misses a game for the Throstles, and has been one of Albion's most consistently reliable players ever since he came to the club in 2004. Jono is one of the most likeable players at The Hawthorns. Don't ask him to go on University Challenge though!

ROBERT KOREN

BORN: 20 SEPTEMBER 1980
POSITION: MIDFIELDER
ALBION APPEARANCES: 62+9 SUB
ALBION GOALS: 11

At just £650,000, buying the Slovenian international has to be one of the best pieces of transfer business Albion have ever done.

Robert took plenty of time to get his first Albion goal but after that, he couldn't stop scoring, getting into double figures as the Throstles headed for the Premiership, playing a big part in that season's success. An energetic presence in midfield and a superb passer of the ball, Roko is ideally suited to playing in the top division.

CHRIS BRUNT

BORN: 14 DECEMBER 1984
POSITION: WINGER
ALBION APPEARANCES: 26+15 SUB
ALBION GOALS: 5

Drafted in from Sheffield Wednesday, the Northern Irish international was a constant menace with his ability to fire in dangerous crosses from any angle and any distance.

His left foot has the same accuracy as a Tiger Woods golf shot, able to pick out anybody in the box at will and place the ball on the spot for them. Took a while to find his very best form but once he had settled into life at The Hawthorns, he was a key member of the promotion team.

FILIPE TEIXEIRA
BORN: 2 OCTOBER 1980
POSITION: MIDFIELDER
ALBION APPEARANCES: 30+7 SUB
ALBION GOALS: 5

Few knew much about the Portuguese midfielder when he signed for Albion in the summer of 2007, but we knew plenty about him by Christmas when he had emerged as one of the most exciting and influential players at the club.

A nasty knee injury cut short his season and he will miss the early stages of the Premier League campaign too, but his value to the team was underlined when his team-mates all wore Teixeira shirts in his honour in the warm up ahead of the final game of the season at Queens Park Rangers.

ROMAN BEDNAR
BORN: 26 MARCH 1983
POSITION: STRIKER
ALBION APPEARANCES: 23+11 SUB
ALBION GOALS: 17

Czech international Bednar joined Albion on loan from Hearts before turning that into a permanent deal after a sensational first season at The Hawthorns where his goals played a big part in Albion's success.

A strong leader of the line who can play on his own up front or alongside a partner, Roman is a great finisher who played a particularly important part in the promotion as Albion's lone striker when Ishmael Miller and Kevin Phillips were out injured.

LUKE MOORE

BORN: 13 FEBRUARY 1986
POSITION: STRIKER
ALBION APPEARANCES: 3+7 SUB

Luke made the short move from Villa Park towards the end of last season and like Roman Bednar, his loan was converted into a permanent transfer in the summer.

Luke followed his brother Stefan into the Villa side where he scored 15 goals in 41 starts for the club. With plenty of pace and an eye for goal, as well as Premier League experience behind him, Moore's quality should prove to be a real asset to the Baggies back in the top flight.

ISHMAEL MILLER

BORN: 5 MARCH 1987
POSITION: STRIKER
ALBION APPEARANCES: 28+12 SUB
ALBION GOALS: 16

Ishmael was a surprise loan signing from Manchester City at the start of last season but his explosive goalscoring form soon established him as a big fan's favourite and his loan became a permanent move in January 2008.

Strong, quick and with a great left foot, he scored some vital goals for the Throstles, not least his hat-trick at Bristol Rovers that put Albion into the FA Cup semi-final at Wembley. Still learning the game, he's likely to give one or two Premier League defences the shock of their lives this season.

DEAN KIELY

BORN: 10 OCTOBER 1970
POSITION: GOALKEEPER
ALBION APPEARANCES: 75

Dean took the Golden gloves award in the Championship last season having posted more clean sheets than any other goalkeeper, a reward which underlined his value to the title winning side where his experience and calming influence on and off the field were important elements in the bigger picture.

Fiercely competitive and ultra professional, Kiely has played more than 750 senior games in his career and shows every sign of having plenty more to add to that tally in the coming seasons, having won his place back in the Irish national side at the end of last season.

GRAHAM DORRANS

BORN: 5 MAY 1987
POSITION: MIDFIELDER
ALBION APPEARANCES: 0

Drafted in from Scottish Division One side Livingston, Graham is seen very much as a player for the future by the Albion coaching staff, but also as someone who is potentially a very good footballer in the making, which is why the club had no hesitation in bringing him south when the opportunity was there.

He was voted the PFA's Player of the Year in Division One last season further confirming his ability, something he will be looking to prove in front of his new employers throughout his season.

MAREK CECH

BORN: 26 JANUARY 1983
POSITION: DEFENDER
ALBION APPEARANCES: 0

Another summer signing, costing
£1.4million from Porto, the left-back is
versatile enough to play either in midfield
or at centre-half while Cech also has
plenty of experience at the top level,
playing in the Champions League for
Porto and on 30 occasions for Slovakia.

He started his career at Inter Bratislava
and then, having won a league title at
Sparta Prague, Marek moved on to Porto
where he carried on in the same fashion,
being part of the league winning side in
each of the last three seasons.

DO-HEON KIM

BORN: 14 JULY 1982
POSITION: MIDFIELDER
ALBION APPEARANCES: 1+6 SUB
ALBION GOALS: 1

The South Korean international joined
Albion on loan initially before the transfer
was made permanent last summer after
he had shown enough quality to suggest
he could make a big contribution to
Albion's Premier League campaign.

Although he was largely on the bench
through the second half of last season, he
made an impressive impact on the FA Cup
semi-final against Portsmouth at
Wembley Stadium and ended the season
with his first Albion goal on the final
afternoon at QPR as the Throstles
clinched the League Championship trophy
at Loftus Road.

MICHAL DANEK
BORN: 6 JULY 1983
POSITION: GOALKEEPER
ALBION APPEARANCES: 0

Czech goalkeeper Michal Danek joined Albion on loan from Plzen last January and spent the second half of the Championship winning season as back up to Dean Kiely. Danek's loan was further extended to the end of 2008 when the club can convert the deal into a permanent transfer.

An imposing 'keeper at 6 feet 4 inches tall, Danek has had to adapt to the English way of playing the game and the different demands it places on goalkeepers but plenty of hard work under Joe Corrigan in training is paying off!

SCOTT CARSON
BORN: 3 SEPTEMBER 1985
POSITION: GOALKEEPER
ALBION APPEARANCES: 0

The England goalkeeper was a summer scoop of a signing for the Throstles, joining from Liverpool for £3.25million, which represents a bit of a bargain for a young goalkeeper who is only going to get better and better.

Carson has performed regularly in the Premier League over the last two seasons, on loan at Charlton Athletic and Aston Villa, but the chance of playing regularly for a permanent club will surely be of further benefit to him as he looks to build his career at club and country level.

GOAL OF THE SEASON

With over 100 to choose from, the 2007/08 Goal of the Season was one of the most closely fought ever.

It was up to Albion fans to select their top strike and the votes poured in to the club's website.

And the winner? Kevin Phillips in the 5-0 rout of Scunthorpe United over Christmas 2007.

Kev had already got himself on the scoresheet with a first half volley, smashed into the top corner from 25 yards, but there was better to come early in the second half.

James Morrison dashed into the box, former Albion 'keeper Joe Murphy came dashing the other way to block the ball out to the edge of the box.

It fell to Phillips who measured an inch perfect chip into the top corner — even Tiger Woods can't chip that well!

QUIZ ANSWERS

WORDSEARCH p7

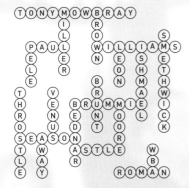

```
P           B           K
H A W T H O R N S       O
I           O   U       R
L   L E O N     O E
L L S T F H T   M   N
I   V C H K L O A   B
P I G R E E N I N G   G
S   L N   N B U N A   E
D   A   I S H M A E L
F   G M V Z X B O M S
R   M O R R I S O N   U
```

BIRD BRAIN! p18

1. Norwich City, the Canaries
2. Crystal Palace, the Eagles
3. Cardiff City, the Bluebirds
4. Sheffield Wednesday, the Owls

CROSSWORD p24

BIG ALBION QUIZ p26

1. Kevin Phillips at Burnley.
2. Chris Brunt at QPR.
3. Preston North End.
4. Preston North End!
5. Republic of Ireland.
6. Middlesbrough.
7. Lee Marshall v Leeds United.
8. 1919/1920.
9. Tony Brown.
10. Kevin Donovan – 1993 play offs.
11. Johnny Giles.
12. Brian Talbot.
13. Chelsea.
14. Stefan.
15. Cyrille Regis, Laurie Cunningham and Brendon Batson.
16. Eric Clapton – Backless.
17. West Bromwich Strollers.
18. 1900.
19. Belgium.
20. Adrian Chiles.

SIGN HERE! p34

1. Filipe Teixeira
2. Neil Clement
3. Sherjill Macdonald
4. Carl Hoefkens
5. James Morrison

MAZE p46